HUNTING

Oliverio Arreola

Translated by Victoria M. Contreras

Las Lenguas de Babel Collection
MEXICAN POETRY IN TRANSLATION

© Oliverio Arreola, 2017
© Translation: Victoria M. Contreras, 2017
© Libros Medio Siglo, 2017

All rights reserved. This book or any portion thereof may not be reproduced or used in any manner whatsoever without the express written permission of the publisher except for the use of brief quotations in a book review.

First Printing 2017

ISBN 13: 978-0-9864497-9-6
ISBN 10: 0-9864497-9-2

Cover Design/Diseño de portada: Victoria Selene Cantú

This publication was made possible with the help of the Translation Support Program (PROTRAD) dependent of Mexican cultural institutions.

Esta publicación fue realizada con el estímulo del Programa de Apoyo a la Traducción (PROTRAD) dependiente de instituciones culturales mexicanas.

www.librosmediosiglo.org
mediosigloeditorial@gmail.com

Harlingen, Texas
USA

PRINTED IN THE UNITED STATES OF AMERICA
IMPRESO EN ESTADOS UNIDOS DE AMÉRICA

HUNTING

HUNTING

For Jazmín Bueno Tapia, for the "I do not believe you";
for the four, the Junes and the 19, the Nobody, the without you,
the without me and the good done. For the spaces of the rooms
that were our hunting ground, the Big House, and for the eight
letters of my name.
And for this White One.

*... I thought of giving myself to the sea
and see the liquid part of the world.*
Herman Melville

The Natural History of Fish

Three are the types of sharks. There are those of a huge size, real and fearsome monsters. [...] One of these species is that of those that have spots on their body and which could be called "thresher sharks". [...] Those with spots on their body have a thin skin and their head is flat, while the others, with strong skin and pointed head, are white.

History of Animals, Claudio Eliano

FIRST IMMERSION

The *White One* is a rock salmon with a black or gray-blue back,
a net-tearing shark with three rows of fangs on the snout
and a thirsty jaw of more than half a meter to
    swallow more than one ocean.
The *White One* is a huge cartilage machinery that
    sails offshore
in an internal sea.
Intense fish, it rows with a ferocious hatred against the sea,
against the light, against its chest and also against himself.
The *White One* is a playful hairless shark, a relentless
    swimmer,
a brutal killer of dry nerves convulsing in
    black blood.
Prey to the harpoon, it neglects its instincts and begins to
    dream among the clouds,
against the solar fire of the gulls, against the precipice's
    chisel sky,
and pursues the flight of the salt and watches the southern course
of the albatrosses.
Animal at last –like me, like us –
always falls wounded, flowing like clouds.

But the *White One* is a White One like seven seas, a white navigator,
an enormous Poseidon of Returns.

LITORAL OF THE BEATS

He tells me to leave. That the North is a garden of wills of sleet and warm water and thick coasts of whiteness like a lawn on grass and like that geography of Greenland without dust, stones or volcanic rock ... He tells me to go. That he will miss me in every green pasture that he finds and in every dry grass of autumn ... He tells me to go. But he does not know. He does not know of the journeys in my mind, of seeing the dawn leaving ..., of arriving in the afternoon, and of tiredness, and seeing the "warm snow" - only warm by his eyes, only warm by his voice - when he tells me to leave.

IN OPEN SEA

The *White One* is not a teleost fish: it sails the world
        without ribs
and with a dark rudder by the greyish blue back.
Fins on the trunk, it is a machine with very precise
        nerves.
But it does not withstand the heat of storms or the temptation
        of hugs.
In the game of love, it loses the iron of its teeth
and surrenders like a salmon to the nets.

But the *White One* is suicidal.
Besides if it is about another *White One*, in female,
more ferocious and more canine,
more mermaid and more lie.

NORTH LAKE

Where are you? What are you doing now? Who misses you in my memory? Who do you bite with the dawn? The streets by the Lake are long and beautiful without your eyes, with bodies of daring boys and devastated women. The Lake is a crystal around fall time, a warm mirror where I throw my questions every afternoon. I know you're not here. The summer evenings turn red in my eyes. They turn yellow ... the leaves of the trees turn dry in my hands. And so, without more, the air, the cold, the snow appear as I pass, and the green meadow burns while you, while I, while the Lake ... Where are you?

SECOND IMMERSION

This *Carcharodon carcharias* loses ground and loses weight.
It is no longer that giant seven meters Polyphemus
       with high jaws and big teeth.
Opened to blood, it drifts around on reefs and scares the people
       on the beach
and looks at the stars in the background and contemplates
another dogfish and squids alike.
Darkened by the dawn
as it hurls itself as it breaks waves every afternoon to wait for the
twilight and the night,
to see a swordfish plough through and to look at the manta ray,
and to hear the dolphin's song at a distance,
and see the dawn appear and the full moon
and even - also, why not? - to remember you.

The *White One* is hungry.
This whiteteeth killer is hungry,
a woman's hunger like the night.

NORTH LAKE. SUMMER

I leave to the Reserve in the morning. First, I walk t through the meadow and avoid the graveyard. Snowflakes hide as I walk. The trees, strange as it may be, shrink their branches because I dream, because I caress each of its leaves as if I miss a corpse. The air is paused by my mouth, seeking to lose itself among the tombs before I breathe it in and return it like a cold north wind. I avoid the graveyard because you always come to my room like a dead man, like an open grave, like a certain mouth when it opens right in the middle of my skin, like a rotten and blind sun. I avoid the cemetery. I do not want to read the eight letters of your name anymore. And I leave to the Reserve in the morning.

SOUTH BEACH

This dogfish breathes sand through the pores while
        sleeping
and wakes up with a sore body.
Bleeding because of a meter and a half harpoon, it lets itself die by
        half nets
and it hurls itself irascibly to the rocks.

Wounded to the vertebrae, it takes its heart out and
        chews it.
It wants to rip off the muscle that hurts, the blood that
        bursts it daily,
and spits against the water and curses it,
and rages against the sea,
and writes its poems with its fists.

This dogfish already hates flowers and is shipwrecked:
no more jasmine in its house,
nor feverish embrace in the storm.

So much sea! So much sea salt in the veins devastates it!
And it goes into the beach looking for another sea to comfort it,
an evergreen, a scentlikeme or another alwaysyourscent:
another fish that it can jump with light at dawn.

LITORAL OF THE BEATS. THIRD STATION

The autumn has an ocher crystal skin. I get up in a checkered gown and curse with my nails and I break you in the mirrors with my eyes. I get in the car and I imagine you coming in my head like a deep river, like a dark fog that does not want to snow. Suddenly everything changes. You become a hunting dog, a bird pecking on my side, in a sharp scream that makes me tremble. Then I open the door and there you are, tucked under the front seat; and the sun burns my hand and a profuse trembling enters against my chest because in the air, because in the light, because in the sky ..., as if suddenly with the wind you also inhabit me. You are always in this thirsty atmosphere in which I breathe. The autumn has an ocher crystal skin ...

TOWARDS THE NORTH

The *White One* is a teleost only by blood, and sails
        the world without ribs
and with a numbed skeleton that runs by miracle
        and without cartilage.

Teleost even in blood, is a silent sevenmeters,
a dust cloud between the shoal, a liquid storm
        in the mud,
an eternal hummingbird, an openoceans.

But this is not a fish. It is a *Carcharodon carcharias*
which takes the salt like a shroud,
and is shakes off the waters--in the inner beach-
and shakes the death that it carries in its ribs,
and it opens inside you, inside me – on us –
and in that burning salt in which you hurt me.

LITORAL OF THE BEATS. WINTER

The cold grows its branches by the house, it goes up through my room, shows off vines, it covers my door with a dark green mold and mullein. It wakes up in the morning, closes my path to grass and evergreens, and paints its complexion green, and it covers my bed of weeds in mud, and my blankets get colder. Its artificial color of landscapes and emeralds is not enough and it demands its pigments, more precise and bitter than algae, sadder than the rain when it rages against the forest. I get up suddenly and I do not see it. I get another blanket and the ice - in my veins - runs deeper inside. The snow falls thicker and whiter by the door, but it scares me when I see that my house is already a single leaf, a silent fern, a vine opening me to the silence, a black forest tied to my questions. The cold grows its branches through my house.

NORTH BEACH. TO THE SEA

The *White One* no longer beats its fins and it turns over face up
   between the waves.
And it embraces, the inner moon, with the swaying of the current.

The *White One* is already dead -they told themselves. -
They saw it chest up brought in by the sea, without fighting
   against the current.
First, beating its fins. Later (almost suffocating or
   suffocated)
moving slowly in an embrace as in an act of
   love towards the clouds.

But the *White One* is not dead. In fact, it was dying.
Not from a harpoon, but from the soul.
Abandoned in the clear waters and to the crackling glow
   of seagulls,
the *White One* looks at the round body of the moon
and it embraces it with its hands
     -I mean, its fins. -

There is no doubt that the *White One* is a romantic!
But with such an extensive sea, with so much ocean salt in its
        veins,
the desire to kill is ethereal,
the desire to kiss, a total ocean.

OCEAN SEA

The bed you left is falling to pieces while I sleep; it eats away at my limbs during the night and it drags my torso by the pelvis. Burning bitch between the sheets, it bites me. And me, during my sleep, scratch her. I struggle against her at point-blank range and I also make her take my barks. But then she gets more furious and bites into the flesh-and even deeper-and it sinks its teeth in sharply, and barks at me tormented by its rage, until it succeeds in waking me up. The bed that you left falls apart while I sleep.

(...)

The *White One* assumes that the North is in the north
and it sets out to look for its compass and sextant.
The gulf is a violent ocean,
a bay half a space of your body and my body,
with dust cloud edges at close range.

I cross my fingers and this fish waves its tail against the
        plankton
moving the rudder by your sides,
and pours through its blood a dioxide that burns its memory
and its storms call it by the blue salt
and travels North.
This fish is a mountain of pollen and phosphide by the water;
a trail of blues and jasmines emanating from it;
a deep-sea flower silence.

ADRIFT ISLAND

It's not Sunday yet. I cross a tunnel. Space clouds the color, the clarity. It is a damp and narrow basement. And I get claustrophobia. Do I cling to the silence, the sky, the wind ... to what? Suddenly, I urge the heat, the stars, the flowers, your voice, your breath; your deep awakening while I kiss you between the sheets and you're not here. The day goes by slowly. Memory betrays me. I say your name. Between laughs and chores I want to stop telling you ..., to stop waiting. I want to sleep, to run away, to get tired. I find that my body hurts more. I know you're not here. I know you never arrive on weekends and yet you are always here. I know that the air, the work, the water, the food ... Everything goes in my mouth like a bullet, a sword or a wound ..., I know that it enters like a never wanting to wake up. It's not Sunday yet. I cross a tunnel.

IRACSIBLE SEA

The angered *White One* fights the reefs,

and attacks the plankton

and the intestinal flora at the depth of the ocean.

It charges and messes them up!

It hits with its tail against the water and it swims furiously with
      its jaws.

And thinks blackly in his ribs.

And it wants to burn the hugs in its fins,

and to open its body like someone who rips his shirt open.

The fish, who is sick with double fins,

has the membranes of its eyes that are rotting

and it becomes angered,

and it fights the reefs,

and attacks the plankton ...

LITORAL OF THE BEATS. FIRST GLACIATION

I shut myself off to sea and sky, to book and music, to whip and storm. And I walk away. And I go to bars and parties and talk on the phone and do yoga at night. But when I get home, the newspaper makes me mad, makes big sores on my body, a tangled being going into delirium. Each word compares you; each act, only one: yours, repeated. I close the book with blank pages in my hands and then I condemn you. Is it you I'm talking to? Or did I speak to a dead person? All this makes me tremble. The snow begins to fall through my house. I have frozen your cry as I have frozen you in the silence. Then I shut myself...

HARPOON TO THE SEA

The *White One* lurks by the coast by the Lake.
It wants to swallow the sand that hinders it, to make its way
        through the mud
and to advance-by bites-
by burning asphalt and cement.

The *White One* wants to pass.
Get rid of the sands already.
Break the buildings.

The *White One* wants to sit and watch the bridges and
        their cables,
and look at the skyscrapers and touch their reefs.

The *White One* wants to breathe the ugly water
-it can no longer open the gills,
nor break in the choking the chest's most thundering
        sighs.-

The *White One* is a numbing sigh,
A half-body harpoon lost in the blood.

OCEAN SEA. POST MORTEM

I know I'll let the phone ring. Let it ring slowly until it tires out. I know that everyone will look at each one of my actions and will ask me not to answer. And I won't. And there will be no need for them to insist. I know that your voice, the one that is there, the one waiting for me behind that lost number, will yell at me while you call me. And it will be filled with wrath. And a wall will rise against you, without rest. And ashes will fall on me and your poems will rise against my face. I know I won't be yours, that I will never be yours, that the ring will not be there anymore. That never more. I know I'll let the phone ring.

HUNTING INSTRUCTIONS

To kill the *White One* requires a little more than a
        caress.
Even to go beyond a kiss in the thawing
kilometers of earth in your body.

The *White One* does not die easily.
Not if there is a guide in the heights that elevates it
and a three-face goddess going up the ocean.
Fin against salt, sun and vinegar, the fish does not die.
And looks for an evergreen, a scentlikeme, or a foreverscent:
In the darkest doubt of its body.

ADRIFT ISLAND. HYPOTHERMIA

I know he's gone crazy. And he calls himself *Blanco*, Oil, Oliv, Oliverio or Eightletters. I know that sometimes he also dreams and is lost in a December that does not exist and in a winter on the Lake. I know that he likes to cover himself with onions, to think like a maiden and to be seen in an unfeeling tuber until tiredness. I know that he goes through the streets repeating the jasmines of the house, stripping the leaves of autumn and grieving the poppies every day in a nearly gray, almost violet, almost purple or almost dark magenta. I know he goes out into the streets in silence to listen to me in the sound; And that he tastes me as I go singing through the air, because his atmosphere is my voice and never dispenses his contact. I know he's going to die. I know he's going to die. Because one night I left him wounded and smelly after having killed him with machetes. I know he's gone crazy.

BLANK WRITING

I

The *White One* has a leaf of jasmine in the whole chest
                because it is *white*,
although others say it is due to swimming too much with a full
                moon.

II

Today there is a new moon.
Yesterday, the other one was dying.
Perhaps in fourteen days this moon will be perfect,
perhaps again it'll die,
perhaps again moon
and never mine.

III

The *White One* swims in the shadows, wanders ..., and gets
impatient in the thicket of its image among the plankton of whales
that eat at night.

The back side up *White One* knows that the blood is a thawing, but swims to the intersection and towards the North. And it wants to go uphill, try other currents, and let other seas give it shade. The *White One* assumes that the sea is a hug and wants to try other waters, other worlds that give it shade between the salt and sediments ... but the sea. Another is the sea: its inner sea.

IV

When you go to the sea, do not say anything.
"I'm not torn to pieces",
nor "I am desperate," and "do not let me go,
      I'm dying."
Don't you see that I'm already shipwrecked in these verses?
Don't you see that in these letters - which today others call
      poems,
to touch you, alone, with them - I restrain myself?

For you.
No more than for you.
The *White One* writes only for you ...It writes in a blank.

EPISTOLARY

I owe you the blue striped shirt that I could not keep for you. And that trip to Uruapan, the past twelfth of December when we saw each other.

I owe you the calendar that we keep and that has been falling apart while alone - with such sadness - time passes.

I owe you the games with my children, the birthdays that we never celebrated together.
I owe you the red scar where you hurt me and you will never heal so you won't suffocate, so I do not get hurt and lonely, and infected and sicker.

I owe you the agony, the slow tale with which you passed my sorrows alone; the breath of the afternoon that still suffocates while I sleep, the brief cold embrace that lies dead between the arms, in which sadly I still sail today.

I owe you everything I gave you, my body that is gone and that you do not have either. I owe it to you. Because if you're not here, perhaps I never gave it to you - or maybe - I never really wanted it to be like I said: always yours.

I owe it to you because today, since you are gone, I'm going crazy, and sometimes deaf and blind, and I contemplate you. And I start to cook to forget you and do the housework, to calm the appetite of your name, so that I stop pronouncing your verses and your letters, cut myself off from your words and forever what one day, I also told you in my heart.

I start cooking so that I think of instructions and recipes, of kilos of your meat and my meat, and of a flour that we never mixed with eggs to make for us those hot cakes that we promised ourselves as we spread honey and marmalade on our hands, and we were dying of diabetes.

I cook so I can cry just as we weep with onions. And it is not my weeping that misses you, but the one of your table that awaits you with tears closed and pressed against the fist, while the chair made a waddle wets the cheeks every day with its eyes, almost dead, because it awaits for you here and you do not come, and it gets tired of looking at its four desolate feet.

I cook for you because, when you left, you told me with your eyes that you were leaving, but also that you would come back and that I did not know how to use a knife or slice the carrots for a salad with those vegetables that one day both of us gathered.

I owe you. I know I owe you.

I owe you the salt and pepper, and the garlic and the onion, and the pinch of cinnamon for the tea with which I keep waiting for you.

I owe you the blue striped shirt ...

MIRRORS

The chest of this fish is a jasmine petal because of the shape and color when it swims upright.
The chest of this fish is a jasmine petal: my milky way.

SCRIVENER'S ROOM

I try to write, but I cannot. A poison enters my back, and it travels through my blood like a worm and ignites its thorns in its path. I try to write, but I cannot. The words get stuck in my hands; They die in my folded nerves. Stuck on walls, they become crucifixes.

I try to write, but I cannot. Perhaps it's because of the cold of the snow, or that of the streets without an ocean, or that of the water without a fish to navigate it.

I try to write, but I cannot. The autumn air turns on even more fierce through my fingernails, and writes more oceans than the house, and that salt pours between the eyes. I try to write, but I cannot. It is written in my blood. There is not a *White* shark for my craving.

HUNTING

The mullet, which is said to control its voracity and to practice temperance [...] Its food is found in dead fish.

History of Animals, Claudio Eliano

COMPASS AND SEXTANT

My North is a jasmine of wills, a velvet silver coated by her eyes.
My North is the thawing of my hands, an iceberg contained between my chest while I sleep.
My North is a north compass when I get up at midnight and in the sky there is a sextant that gives directions.
My North is a thirsty bird, a bird that indicates new land in every trip that I undertake towards myself.
My North is this waiting in impatience, numb because the dream is a rodent of wills.
My North is another north that dreams of me in the Reserve, or between a Cemetery and with a Lake.
My North is always a moon that I summon at midnight, a flower of five moons like petals, a flower of five thoraxes when I speak to you.
My North: the six letters of your name.

NORTH HUNTING

The male's skin is not as thick and will break if it hunts between corals, even if it frequents the sea urchins. The skin of the male is of timid signs: cartilage in the fin, nerves in the chest; it carries a sensor to know which female will injure it. Its skin, thin to the point of astonishment, tears easily; More so if it is attacked by a female. Machoskin even in the blood, it tans with salt and sun, in open sea, and sighs with pain in the mid-afternoon, with its lateral eyes face down and sighing fins up in the air. In its strange still sea, the machoskin gazes at the sea for itself.

        And it advances.

In the soul it takes another sea (also its doubt). A sea darker than the night.

HUNTING

The bite of a female is deadly from the teeth; more so if it comes from within and is hungry and thirsty, and seeks a male from afar.
The bite of a female is deadlier if it arrives alone and - love between the teeth - releases the blow on the male.
The bite of a female can break all the bones, but never touches the heart: the prey never dies.
The bite of a female is marked, as if wanting to leave in it the reason for its existence.
The bite of a female is always disproportionate, mathematical and perfect.
The bite of a female is completely absurd: three hundred times greater than the bite of any man or mine.
The bite of a female occurs with strong jaws
-with brackets, if you can-to bleed a lifetime.
The bite of a female *white* shark is like yours: to know that you are here, that you are still alive and you always hurt.

BOOK OF JONAH

... and Jonah was in the belly of the fish
three days and three nights.
Jonah, 2: 1

I. JONAH. SONG

I want to travel. To run away. May my flesh be of the way.

II. JONAH. FIRST DAY

I know it's daytime because at night the shark does not swallow fish, and it settles with its belly up and its caudal fin stays still. I know it's daytime because the fish's peace is not an uneasiness not even a sea urchin encircles my rib.

      I know it's daytime and I sleep. To doubt, the night remains.

III. JONAH'S FIRST NIGHT

I go inside a fish like the night. My night is darker than doubt.

IV. JONAH. SECOND DAY

In the distance, I am not. I am he and he is my doubt. In the distance, I am filled with questions, I choose my jealousy well, I demolish the enthusiasm. In the distance, the silt gets muddy and those black algae become vomit. At night, tired of waiting for you, a blood taste like the tremble of a wound overcomes me and I sink my teeth and nails in this white shark as I burn. I know I'm going inside a fish into the nets. I know that this love for him is captive of his blood, is a tired one of waiting for him, a breathing sea urchin ..., a slowly getting maggoty every night.

V. JONAH'S SECOND NIGHT

I know I'm in you because you sail with a course defined only by chance and surprise. The night is so dark because I know you are swimming and because I get dizzy inside. Carrying a fish inside is like pulling the heart out, taking off a rib, swimming flush with fire in deep sea lavas. I carry an angry anesthetized *White One* and he carries me in his inner depths.

VI. IN MEDIAS RES

I know I'm in you because I'm sailing. I know I'm in you because you doubt me. I know I am in you because I navigate and because I do not have a heart to think of you, nor puffing air alveoli to breathe more blood, if in tachycardias I spread out.

I know I'm in you because I'm sailing. I know I'm in you because you doubt me. You, doubt. My doubt: the queen of all mothers.

VII. JONAH. THIRD DAY

Harpoon up, cartilage open, I run out of air in the lungs. Loving is a lure for grief. The mourning, the anesthetized step of death. My body rots at night; at daytime, the rage and the spits of my flesh ferment. Anxiety and thirst and only salt like an ointment in my ribs. I think the day. It's just like the night. As dark also as doubt is.

VIII. JONAH'S THIRD NIGHT

During the day, the fish does not lie. I go deep inside it and I know it loves me. Its patience is the patience of an ocean, a great waving against the rock and rough water. During the day, the fish does not lie. Its salts do not hurt and I slowly breathe the reef's light, its tropical waters, its warm blood that in the hands accompanies me. Belly in the air, I know that I am inside the fish and I am also another fish deep inside this one. A breathing without you, without me; without me and without you and a little without us. I communicate to the fish that my heart beats if it bites me. In every dark night, beats and fish are one. Beats to the fish. Do you feel me?

IX. ON THE BANKS OF NINEVEH

I will no longer throw my body into the carrion.

What else won't love be when it is not reciprocated?

X. IN MEDIAS RES II

Now therefore, O LORD, I beseech thee to slay me; Because death is better to me than life.

Jonah, 4: 3

I will not die by you.
I swim against doubt and against the ground.
And against the sea and against the voice and against
      myself.

I will not die by you.
My body and the salt skin deep in me that already burst tell me.
And the night -on my rib- already darker.

I will not die by you.
My doubt is already great.

FISH IMMERSION

*Everything collapses and I rot,
everything is perishing in my hands.*
José Gorostiza

INTERNAL COMBUSTION

I

Hidden in the corner of the dream, between plankton and intestinal flora, the fish looks like a live tuber and in a lethargic stage. It goes into a break with its listless eyes but it does not sleep: it only dreams. Its eyes covered by membranes, it watches the area of the subsoil and remains in lethargy and levitates one and a half meters between the algae. But in the water that is a worn-out metaphor to define the state of a shark when kissing or after the Iloveyous. Red in combustion, this animal burns inward, and - internal stove, candle flame - burns.
The fish,
        in this state,
                trembles.

II

The night is a hand for those who follow the night.
                                    Edmond Jabès

The fish waits between the silence of the waves and drifts when it is late, the tide rises and the current begins.

Moon fish on the belly and soot on the loin, it submerges and no one gives a penny for its insides, not even for its rich liver in oils.

At night, with its chest up, it camouflages with the moon. But in its dream of embracing her, it does not see her. Its lateral eyes lose her when grasping her.

To love the moon is an illusion, a waste of time. Love is an oppressive fountain, an overwhelming embrace by the pores. If you ask, what is love? To love the moon is silence, a fiery leap of three meters that breaks the skeleton of a shark. You would have to love blindly, with your eyes on your back and to embrace that which cannot be embraced. And to feel the warm waters of the tropics or a cold front that unleashes the storm. You would have to love blindly, in the night and at a distance, and wait - with what patience! – for the tide to rise, to jump a little more and reach it.

    To love the full moon is to love blindly. Love, a breathable oasis at night.

III

The fish's patience is twelve hours, because it waits for the night while it sleeps.

It does not eat. And it hunts not for its prey, but for the waiting. And it repeats the hook day by day, with its imminent term, to which it always arrives punctual, in an hour.

The fish's patience is twelve hours, because it waits for the tide to rise to jump up a little higher and reach the moon in an embrace. It wants to contain it in the center of its chest, because it knows that it is half gray and half white and longs for - like her - to be round, white also on both sides and also, why not? almost perfect.

The fish makes its way from the bottom and opens the ocean with the tip of its jaws, and throws itself three or four meters in the air, and repeats the jump to exhaustion like an absorbed dance, like an acrobat in the wind. It emerges from the waters like a spear, and bends three or four meters because of its weight. Teleost's gaze, it advances from the bottom and contains the thin breath and does not breathe. From the water it knows that in the air there is another dream: the moon of its embrace, its other sight.

IV

The moon wants foolishness from the *White One*.

As if jumping or embracing her from the water wasn't already a suicide.

To fall from such a leap can break the heart, break the backbone.

Once the *White One* dreamed that it embraced her, that it felt the moon on its fins. But it was just a wrong meteor, a comet bursting through the sky, a huge stone lit in space.

The moon wants the *White One*, but not its teleost's grayish blue.

She, enamored of her reflection - the *White One* is nothing more than a vanity in love - assumes that the chest of the shark is her guide at night that allows her to cross the sea swimming and never drown.

She, in love, demands a target to the *White One*; its heart, its inner sea.

INTERNAL IMMERSION

Yesterday, the fish fell asleep among the rocks. It suffered from tachycardias and huge bites. Abandoned like a shipwreck, it almost caught a hypothermia with the wind and the morning dew.

The fish always dreams. Always on the pillow. But for it, the dream is a sharp pain on the edge of the rocks.

Sometimes it wakes up, because of that suffocating cold, shivering from cramps burning in its hands, and it is frightened and clutches its hands against asphyxiation and drowning. And it takes its chest, flexing its fins to the limit. Something kills it: a vascular attack, a direct biting blow in the myocardium.

When it dreams-already in the course of the pillow-a volcano, a lightning, a whimper: a storm ... comes and awakens him. And it is no more than a weigh anchor or a whipping surf between the rocks.

Gangrene even in the blood, the fish does not dream. It is a corpse that sails through the night.

AQUARIUM

Flee, my beloved;
[...] on the mountains of aromas.
Song of Solomon 8:14

[α] DEFINITIONS (JASEMIN)

Jasmine is a flower of five petals, my perfect compass if I sail with a solar star to the north as a course. Jasmine is a mooned flower, a perfume I chase when I get lost and I do not find the north. Open-sky flower-flower inside-, at night it is a white and grayish fish, with the chest a burning salt, a salt of fire; A lunar flower with a fish inside, but dark.

[β] SPECIES (YASAMIN)

This flower is a pistil, an aquatic reflection and a goddess of three phases, underworld, ethereal and anaerobic. Jasmine in the air becomes moon, mother-of-pearl, shell to the sea and satellite in the water when in the stems the roots dry and wants to graft in the trunks of another sea or another ocean. White petals, it rips-like a champion with his three-meter jumps on the weekends-and goes dark for periods of twenty-eight while it sleeps. Flower to the sea, it opens between white leaves and huggable eyes, and gives itself to my body in perfect communion: its other vegetation, that is of its species.

[γ] INSIDE PASSION (GESSAMIN)

Jasmine grows on the walls of my house. It is a vine that covers my walls, a white cloud if it blooms in the summer, a fresh perfume when it loves me from the depths and just to the north. I inhale it in and it shines through my mouth like a flowered pollen, and it roots down my body, and it grows like a tree by my smell, and it bites deep inside like a shark in love, and like a magma crater that alone bursts on my tongue at night. It grows like that..., and becomes germ, and grows roots and stem, tegument, dry leaf, a time flower in life. Flower in the chest I breath it. And you...Do you smell it?

[δ] GREENHOUSE (GESMIL)

A fish is a pistil that sails in the ocean of a garden: tunas and storms, creeping octopuses, fresh leaf turtles and stem whales. The fish between rosemary and flowers of chimera, wraps up with the shells and looks at the jellyfish, and adorns its white complexion of coral while it hunts me. The fish, always the fish, looking for its garden at the bottom of the ocean.

[ε] GRAFT (GERAMI)

The fish is a flower garden in water, a cartilage thirsty for flesh and evergreens, a navigating nerve that reacts against pollen, at the heat of the brush and the bottom of the ocean. Fish of flowers and bites and carnivorous greens, it moisturizes itself in the wax and embraces the grafts. The fish looks for the root in the stem, the sap, the stem, the ripe fruit in its bite, the sediment pollen, its precise and caste flower, and the incomparable perfume that already flows through its veins. The perfume of a flower is two bloods: yours and mine. And one.

[ζ] SAP (GESMIR)

The sap of the jasmine stains like blood because it is dark in the stalk, a nettle that removes each splinter in vena cava. The sap of the jasmine is a white sun, a moon that turns yellow in the thorax of my blood, a poison between the tongue if it bites me. The sap of the jasmine: the fragments of the body when you tell me: "in your absence I break," "do not let me go, for I will die." The sap of the jasmine, the most ardent night of my blood.

[η] SMELL (JASMINE)

The jasmine flower is a star that gets irritated with internal fire like a blooming magma ..., and follows its swimming course filling up my hugs. Its body is a perfume in which I navigate, a silent iceberg plowing my arteries. Its branches become blood, aromas if I touch them; its flowers - when I talk to it - become White, dark night and more storm and a clot. The dawn strolls by my nose and I discover the hard opium that destroys me while I sleep. Its aroma becomes a splinter, silence, gold, fire. Its smell is a perfume in which I sail; its heart, my tegument in vena cava.

[θ] NAVIGATIONS (ACEMIN)

Erosion is a sea that navigates through my skin. The flower, this vegetative silence that jumps me and shatters dawns. Its corolla of breathless moons gets rid of five fish. *Carcharon carcharias* born of the petiole, and it fixes its jaws in its scent, and pours its conquest on the substance that nests between its leaves, and it poisons all smell, and trusts its perfume as it does the gray amber of the whale.

In its ancient garden, in the painting or in the vase, this flower knows it is ethereal. Not because it's a flower, but because of the seven-seas pollen that leaves the fish swimming in the stars.

LAST GARDEN. LOT'S FLOWER

The dry garden, it is that blood of yours that smells like
    dust.
The dry garden, it is this bright lunar pollen in the morning
    dew.
The dry garden, it becomes a fossil of selachian between the
    saltysea and the saltyocean.
The dry garden, it is bright lunar pollen in the dew of
    the leaves.
The dry garden, statue of salt, the fish looks up.
The dry garden, statue of salt, fish.
The dry the garden, statue of salt.
The dry garden.
Statue.

WHITE ONE TO THE SEA

And I fought against the sea all night,
from Homer to Joseph Conrad,
to reach your desert face
and to read in its sand not to await anything,
not to expect mystery, not to wait.

Gilberto Owen

I.

Stranded on the open sea, on the waves, satellite in the sky, finally the moon comes down and touches the *White One* with her nails.

And, countercurrent love, she spawns it, turns it salt – with lime and earth and granite - and leaves it burning in the water. This fish is a White One in love, with no more fins than its eyes, with no more water flow than the heart, and paddling with its guts.

Animal with pectoral fins, it becomes moon by its house, vessel, sun, sea, utensil, winged garden ..., a poetry collection cutting without direction.

II.

The moon, mirror of volcanic rock, mortar and sea of sand,
   gets undressed.
She puts on her granite towel, and I dry her hair with my
   hands.
Sea salt, white and clear skeleton, cartilage of thirst,
today's moon has ghosts: spurs that bite
   through the chest.
Today's moon is this absence. This not being here that
   bleeds her.
This not being here in the one I am, and in the one I am hiding.
This not being.
This not being.

Close your eyes:
   Do you feel it?

HIGH TIDE

I. Born

The moon swirls around the seashore of her epidermis by my eyes, while I dream like a fish swimming deep sea: open love.

II. Changing

The faithful, the changing, the lunatic, the monthly, the one
   who is reborn and dies, is a goddess of three faces, a flower with
   sleepless compasses.
Craters in the bottom, she shows off stains and sharks
   swimming by ether.
The flame moon, crackling flame.
High flame, white flame, it darkens.
Do you remember that stain I once loved?
It was a moon, and never white.

III. Growing

The moon has grown tonight.
It has grown a little more, but inwards.

SINGING OF THE BLIND

The dolphin sings. They say it's an heir to sirens and can kill a shark with its call.

The dolphin can - the female dolphin - open its body and separate its two bloods (its own and the one of love: the poisoned one), and let it bleed in the Middle Ages style (or a heart surgery, with anesthesia and everything, operating room, scalpel) open chest, and leave it as new, beating at one hundred twenty per minute, ready to love (to kill the heart again, in a crazy arrhythmia and without rest) and to abandon itself to new wounds in the blood.

The dolphin can - the female dolphin - save it, if she wants to, from its blood; to tie him again to its diseased molecule and take it a cocktail of vitamins, in an infinite and irreparable love, and take care of it - as always - with fin and song, with music and storm.

The dolphin can - the female dolphin - camouflage at night on a full moon, and go down to its bedroom, and change the bandages of the wound while singing. It is not a dream being a moon or being female in a dolphin. Nor confuse her with a siren. Singing is, in itself, a thirsty music.

SEA HUNTING

The *White One* is a rainbow of three bloods.
A white swirl of plankton and shoal swimming
        the hemisphere.
The *White One*, blind and deaf, bites its fins as
        it can and, suicidal,
attacks a group of whales
and enraged throws itself at eighteen
-better nineteen- dolphins altogether.

It knows about its death before the trip.

It does not want this blood that kills it.
The *White One* wants a moon to save it from this thirst
        for spiders.
How to drink that animal of open sky in the
        foam of the blood?
How to drink the fresh moon in the morning?
How to drink itself?
If in the sullen blackness is the night.

OPEN SEA

The White One is sleepy and today falls asleep.
    No. There are no clouds in the air.
Silver root, the water – more silver- is blackened with the crescent. Because the moon, if it is not full, misses the eclipses, absorbs the tide and makes storms with the dust.
    The moon, the water well of my body, gravitates to the North and sheds its beats.
    But the *White One*, skeptical in the blood, cold-blooded selachian, anesthetized, needs a ray of sunshine to catch fire and sail upstream upwardnorth.
The *White One* always plays suicide. But in its impious leap it has learned not to kill itself, to cut the water, already closing its snout and falling sideways.
    This *White One* has a hole in the ribs and a death that does not commit suicide.
    And it looks for a sea that reaches farther on this earth.
A sea is a harpoon, a real sharkkiller just north and up to the ice.
    The *White One* wants a sea for its house, a *White One* with crested fins and blue striped shirt ... And it does not want to kill himself.
    To die the night remains.

EULOGY OF THE FISH

The *White One* is white because of life
and not because of the bite that it keeps between its three-
hundred-kilograms teeth as it advances.
Salt on the skin,
It does not allow it to penetrate through its veins, nor to get into
      its tissues,
nor that they kill it at close range,
It does not even play to see itself from afar,
nor does it look at the exact clock of the sun in the west,
nor does it allow the high surge of the sea enraged
      in the storm.
The Southern *White*, with its threatening dorsal fin,
looks to the North for
the shores of bathers kicking.
It approaches and frolics as one who sings to the sea urchins,
and looks for the pier and the fresh beach air
which is not easily found in the deep sea.
The *White One* wants feet to sit,
to cross the fins if possible
and contemplate the sea from the earth.
The *White One* would like to jump like the dolphin off the
      coast,
to diverge from the menacing iron of the harpoon

and from the choral screaming of bathers.
But it is a dream.
As soon as the *White One* is seen, sirens sound,
and the sea wallows among the algae,
in a mad rage that burns their howls.
But the *White One* swims warm, slow, asleep,
with its heart hungry-and it is not of hunger-
with anger in the air-and it is not revenge.-
The *White One* wants the sea to reach its other house:
full moon selachian jasmine,
and look for an April of March, *white* female,
and to take it a blue striped shirt.
The *White was* told that the North was in the Lake,
and that in the North the whole "I do not believe you" gets
                                        [frozen.
And it wants to give that other *White One*
                -the *white* female-
a little of the heat that freezes it
and the most accurate iceberg that hugs him.
But this *White One*
is just a harmless fish,
A sevenmeters with mask of fire,
a shadow refracted by the water,
and some stoneeating teeth that are distressed
because there is no sea beyond the seawall, nor between

                    the docks.

The fish in the *White* sevenseas, a teleosteo blue-gray

                    heart,

an implacable Poseidon of Returns.

ABOUT THE AUTHOR

Photo by Pedro Félix Macedo Aguilar

Oliverio Arreola (Villa de Allende, Mexico, 1974) holds a degree in Latin American Literature from the Universidad Autónoma del Estado de México and a doctorate in Literary Studies. He has been a Fellow of the Fund for the Culture and the Arts of the State of Mexico (FOCAEM) in the areas of poetry and essay.

His publications include *Las otras caras del rostro*, 1998; *Pasión de caza* (Young Poetry Prize José María Heredia y Heredia, 2003); *Mar Adentro*, (National Floral Games of Cd. Del Carmen Poetry Prize, 2009); Cacerías, (Amado Nervo National Poetry Prize, 2011);

and *Caza de ciervo*, 2015. His book *La isla de los pájaros* obtained the Laura Méndez de Cuenca State Literature Prize in 2016. He is currently a professor of Poetry and Creative Writing in the College of Humanities at the Universidad Autónoma del Estado de Mexico. This volume of poetry will captivate the reader with its originality, imagery and humanity.

ABOUT THE TRANSLATOR

Dr. Victoria M. Contreras is a retired Professor of Linguistics and Pedagogy of Language in the Department of Modern Languages and Literatures at the University of Texas-Pan American, also serving as interim director thereof in 2000-2001. She graduated from the University of Texas at Austin where she received her doctorate in Education of Foreign Languages. Throughout her teaching career she has lectured in the United States and Spain. She is widely recognized in the field of applied linguistics, particularly for her research on Spanish for heritage speakers. As a translator she has collaborated with local and national institutions such as the Boys Club, International Airport of Mc Allen, the municipalities of Pharr, Edinburg and McAllen, University of Texas-Pan American, as well as law firms and hospitals. In the field of literary translation, she edited the English translation of *El Corazón Transfigurado/ The Transfigured Heart* (Libros Medio Siglo, 2013) and translated into English the poems *Callejón Kashaní / Kashani Alley, Nunca quise detener el tiempo/I Never Wanted to Stop Time, Reducido a polvo/Reduced to Dust, Cacerías/Hunting, Theory of Losses* and many others.

ÍNDEX

NATURAL HISTORY OF THE FISH

First Immersion 13

Litoral of the Beats 15

In Open Sea 16

North Lake 17

Second Immersion 18

North Lake. Summer 19

South Beach 20

Litoral of the Beats. Third Station 21

Towards the North 22

Litoral of the Beats. Winter 23

North Beach. To the Sea 24

Ocean Sea 26

(...) 27

Adrift Island 28

Irascible Sea 29

Litoral of the Beats. First Glaciation 30

Harpoon to the Sea 31

Ocean Sea. Post Mortem 32

Hunting Instructions 33

Island Adrift. Hypothermia 34

Blank Writing 35

Epistolary 37

Mirrors 40

Scrivener's Room 41

HUNTING

Compass and Sextant 45

North Hunting 46

Hunting 47

BOOK OF JONAH

I. Jonah. Song 51

II. Jonah. First Day 51

III. Jonah's First Night 51

IV. Jonah. Second Day 52

V. Jonah's Second Night 53

VI. In Medias Res 54

VII. Jonah. Third Day 55

VIII. Jonah's Third Night 56

IX. On the Banks of Nineveh 57

X. In Medias Res II 58

FISH IMMERSION

Internal Combustion 61

I 61

II 62

III 64

Internal Immersion 66

AQUARIUM

[α] Definitions (jasemin) 69

[β] Species (yasamin) 70

[γ] Inside Passion (gessami) 71

[δ] Green House (gesmil) 72

[ε] Graft (gerami) 73

[ζ] Sap (gesmir) 74

[η] Smell (jasemin) 75

[θ] Navigations (acemin) 76

Last Garden. Lot's Flower 77

WHITE ONE TO THE SEA

I 81

II 82

High Tide 83

Singing of the Blind 84

Sea Hunting 85

Open Sea 86

Eulogy of the Fish 87

www.ingramcontent.com/pod-product-compliance
Lightning Source LLC
Chambersburg PA
CBHW051659040426
42446CB00009B/1216